# QUALIFIED

HOW TO THINK ABOUT

YOUR MINISTRY EXPERIENCE

IN RELATION TO YOUR JOB SEARCH

## JEFF EADS

MUNCIE
FELLOWS

Cover & design by Carolyn Frost.
Author photo by besweetlight.com

Edited by Dan Daugherty.

ISBN: 978576589524
Imprint: Independently published

# ENDORSEMENTS

Years ago when transitioning from a career as a suburban pastor to a new vocation in New York City, I tended to think of my ministry résumé as a liability. *Qualified* by Jeff Eads provides an antidote to such defeatist thinking. He conclusively demonstrates that those of us who have served in ministries are experts in the top eight skills employers seek. This reframing of our work history provides the vocabulary and confidence we need to seek God's next assignment in the wider world of work. I highly recommend this resource.

**Dr. Chip Roper**
Founder and President, Voca Center and Managing Partner, RKE Partners

We are so grateful for Jeff's insight and expertise. Because our campus staff are not experts in the world of career counseling, they have benefited from Jeff's guidance in helping translate students' ministry experience into language that any employer would understand in a résumé or interview. Armed with the thoughts in *[Qualified]*, our staff have been able to confidently recruit students into ministry opportunities that we know will develop them beyond their investment in campus ministry.

**Chris McComb**
Regional Director, The Navigators

My friend, Jeff Eads, has a lifetime of experience helping people think through questions related to their faith and vocation. Thankfully, Jeff has now stewarded all of that experience, honed through countless personal interactions, into this valuable resource that is available to us all. *Qualified* will help anyone who has been involved in ministry efforts understand the value of that experience and apply it to their job search. What an empowering tool! I hope this resource will inspire countless Christians to pursue God's vocational calling on their life in ways that glorify Him and bless their workplaces.

**Michael Wear**
Founder of Public Square Strategies, LLC
Author of *Reclaiming Hope: Lessons Learned in the Obama White House About the Future of Faith in America*

Solid, practical advice…this is what I wish someone had given me at the start of my career.

**Hugh C. Whelchel**
Executive Director, The Institute for Faith, Work & Economics
and author of *How Then Should We Work?*

*Qualified* is a small but mighty resource for college students and young professionals. Jeff provides important insight to help guide those looking for help considering what's next. He addresses eight competencies with theological depth and practical help that not only help readers take the next step, but live a lifetime of faithfulness in their careers.

**Dr. Drew Moser**
Co-author, *Ready or Not: Leaning into Life in Our Twenties* and Author, *The Enneagram of Discernment: The Way of Vocation, Wisdom, & Practice*

Finally!! A translation guide that can help young (or not so young) Christians translate their ministry experience into language describing qualities, characteristics, skills and experiences that employers are searching for.

And it isn't just the translation. It's the understanding that what I've experienced and learned is directly transferable to the competencies the employer is seeking. That's a confidence builder!

Additionally, it helps the job seeker stay away from language that will repel or confuse the interviewer—"mission trips, Bible study, VBS" and the like can be interpreted as overly religious, narrow minded, intolerant, isolationist, or even weird.

The competencies developed in Christian service activities are directly transferable to secular job opportunities, but language is all-important in communicating these competencies. Communication is a critical life skill, and this short work reveals significant and practical insights in developing that skill.

**BJ Hess**
SVP Global Operations (Retired), Arrow Electronics, Inc.
Chair of the Board, Cairn University

I am a physician, researcher and writer at Mayo Clinic. I am also a committed Christian. As it happens, my most valuable research analyst has a background in ministry and continues to shepherd a congregation part-time. I've never really been able to describe exactly what makes his skillset so valuable. Now I know. *Qualified* now gives me that vocabulary. Every year my program manager screens applications of hundreds of undergraduates and recent graduates, looking for talented young people. We are looking for students with curiosity, passion for research, and an ability to work in teams. Unfortunately, the intangibles that it takes to work in teams, navigate ambiguity, discern next steps in research, or manage conflict in a work environment do not have easily translatable CV categories. That's why I found *Qualified* so intriguing. This is a rare explicit treatment of the intangibles that ministry experience brings to recent graduates. Emotional intelligence, managing team dynamics, comfort in small and large group presentations are just a few of the features we screen for and that are explicitly validated in the brief monograph. The brief entries herein offer accessible summaries that lend practical insights for translating the language of gospel service to the more instrumental, pragmatic, and efficient vocabulary of employers. The Gospel does speak in terms of human capital, but rather giving our bodies as living sacrifices. Lofty, intimidating stuff. But as it turns out, Kingdom work is formative and in ways that it behooves even a greedy employer to consider. Selfless service—the way of Jesus—shapes cultures and work environments; that is indeed attractive, at least for employers with a longer view of success. I highly recommend *Qualified* as a tool to help recent graduates translate their experience to real-world competencies.

**Jon Tilburt, MD**
Professor of Medicine and Biomedical Ethics,
Mayo Clinic Alix School of Medicine, Scottsdale, AZ

# CONTENTS

Acknowledgements . . . . . . . . . . . . . . . . . . . . . . . . . . . . . . . . . . . . . . . . . . *ix*

INTRODUCING THE COMPETENCIES:
How to Make Ministry Experience Matter in Any Job . . . . . . . . . . . . . . . . .1

COMPETENCY ONE: Thinking & Problem Solving . . . . . . . . . . . . . . . . .5

COMPETENCY TWO: Oral & Written Communications . . . . . . . . . . . . . . . .9

COMPETENCY THREE: Teamwork/Collaboration . . . . . . . . . . . . . . . . 13

COMPETENCY FOUR: Digital Technology . . . . . . . . . . . . . . . . . . . . . . 17

COMPETENCY FIVE: Leadership . . . . . . . . . . . . . . . . . . . . . . . . . . . . 21

COMPETENCY SIX: Professionalism/ Work Ethic . . . . . . . . . . . . . . . . . . 25

COMPETENCY SEVEN: Career Management . . . . . . . . . . . . . . . . . . . . . 29

COMPETENCY EIGHT: Global/Intercultural Fluency . . . . . . . . . . . . . . . . 33

CONCLUSION: Where to from here? . . . . . . . . . . . . . . . . . . . . . . . . . . . 37

# ACKNOWLEDGEMENTS

This reflection guide was originally written as a series of individual blog posts for the Muncie Fellows.* I am grateful for the efforts of Adam Bouse and Andrea Eads for reading and providing editorial feedback for the original posts, Bj Hess and others who read and provided feedback along the way, and for Dan Daugherty's editorial work that further refined this present version.

These pages were motivated by years of conversations with university students and professionals who were unaware of the value of the vital competencies that they had developed during their time serving in various ministry contexts. While the principles and examples shared here are ministry focused, they are applicable to any field. The subtitle could easily have been *How to think about your [fill in the blank] experience in relation to your job search.* I appreciate each individual who has entrusted me with your story over the years. I hope that I have helped you share it with a little more clarity.

*Muncie Fellows is a part of the The Fellows Initiative, a network of Christian leadership and vocational development programs for recent college graduates.*

# INTRODUCING THE COMPETENCIES

## HOW TO MAKE MINISTRY EXPERIENCE MATTER IN ANY JOB

**AS A CAREER COACH AT** a state university, I regularly have students from Christian ministries come into my office for résumé reviews and practice interviews. During these conversations, they struggle to translate their experiences at their campus ministries into transferable life skills. They often ask, "What does leading this Bible study have to do with a job?" or, "Does this international ministry trip add any value to my résumé?" The answer is, as it nearly always is, "Yes it's valuable, but you have to talk about it in the language that is relevant to the employer."

Let me give a quick example. An education major lists, "Led a Bible study" on her résumé for a public school job. That school, likely, is not looking for a Bible study leader. However, they are looking for teachers who have experience creating curriculum and lesson plans, teaching, managing group dynamics, and who can create a flyer advertising upcoming events. Did you do any of those things as part of leading your Bible study? Yes? Well great, say that.

I realize that this is a fairly simplistic example and some situations will call for more nuance, but the fact remains: the skills that you have gained in ministry are often transferable to an employer's needs. In fact, they are the eight secret ingredients for which the employer is looking. Well, maybe the ingredients themselves are no secret, but the fact that these transferable skills are part of the very fabric of a biblical worldview and ministry experience seems to be one.

I am going to let you in on these not-so-secret ingredients (referred to throughout as "competencies" and "transferable skills"). Then I will provide practical examples of how you may have already developed these through your ministry experiences and how you can articulate these throughout your job search. But first, let me say this: the source that identified these eight transferable skills is legit and based on national research.

The National Association of Colleges and Employers (NACE) is the leading source of information on the employment of the college-educated, as well as hiring and trends in the job market. They track starting salaries, recruiting and hiring practices, as well as student attitudes and outcomes. NACE reports that "the career readiness of college graduates is an important issue in higher education, in the labor market, and in the public arena." They have developed a definition of career readiness, based on extensive research among employers, and identified eight competencies that indicate a person's preparedness for the workforce. *(https://www.naceweb.org/career-readiness/competencies/career-readiness-defined/)*

It would be discouraging to find out that these eight competencies were specific skills that are achievable only by uniquely gifted individuals (e.g. "Must be knowledgeable of xyz software development...and love calculus") or that the competencies somehow contradicted your personal values (e.g. "Must be willing to prioritize work over personal life at all cost"). The good news is that these competencies directly align with a biblical worldview:

1. Critical Thinking & Problem Solving
2. Oral & Written Communications
3. Teamwork/Collaboration
4. Digital Technology
5. Leadership
6. Professionalism/Work Ethic
7. Career Management
8. Global/Intercultural Fluency

*In the following chapters we will consider the definitions that NACE provides of these competencies and how they are developed in Christian ministry.*

# FOR REFLECTION

The job search process is all about storytelling. Cover letters, résumés, answers to interview questions, networking—each of these tell part of your story. Take a minute and write down a few stories that you might want to tell. Don't worry about writing the whole story now; simply write some topics. *Here are some examples:*

1. *Led a small group*
2. *Attended a leadership training*
3. *Spring break missions trip*
4. *RA in the resident hall*
5. *Help in the children's Sunday school*

# COMPETENCY
# ONE

## CRITICAL THINKING & PROBLEM SOLVING

*"Exercise sound reasoning to analyze issues, make decisions, and overcome problems. The individual is able to obtain, interpret, and use knowledge, facts, and data in this process, and may demonstrate originality and inventiveness."* *

**THIS IS WHAT I HEAR** from employers all of the time when I ask them about this skill: "We need people who, when they run into a problem, think through the issue, come up with a few solutions, and bring them back. For example, *Solution A will get the job done more quickly but cost more. Solution B will take an additional week but save us $4000.* We are finding that our younger employees run into obstacles and then come back to management to ask 'What should I do now?' Management doesn't have time to come up with every solution."

Now on the one hand, you were born to do this.

Seriously, the first time that you were ever hungry, what did you do? Cried. What happened next? You were fed. Ever touch a hot stove? Did you do it again? See, you are a natural problem solver. But of course, everybody has that same foundation. Your ministry experience has built upon those instincts in ways that you may have never considered.

* naceweb.org/career-readiness/competencies/career-readiness-defined/

My most substantial critical thinking training came while pursuing a degree in biblical studies. I was faced with the task of examining an ancient text, written in an ancient time, to an ancient culture, by a person who has long been dead. Then I was supposed to make sense of that text and present it to a contemporary audience, using contemporary vocabulary. I was then to provide a timeless truth to that audience while hopefully keeping them from dying of boredom. If I came across an agricultural term that I didn't know, like *yoke*, I had to look it up and then figure out what it meant. I had to ask questions like, "What's the big deal about the dad of the prodigal son hiking up his man-dress thing and running to his son? Is that some kind of cultural thing?" Not only is critical thinking necessary to our spiritual development, but it also is a key work skill. (In fact, *all* of the liberal arts help to develop critical thinking skills; that's one reason that they are SO important.)

While Bible study is a foundational skill for a Christian leader, it is certainly not the only transferable skill. Much like other student organizations, campus ministries develop problem-solving skills in a number of other ways; you just need to learn how to talk about them.

Have you ever led a small group? What happened when the meeting time didn't work for some of your members? How did you resolve the issue? Did you ever market the group to others through fliers or personal invitations? Did you create a fun and welcoming environment by providing snacks? Did your group have an end of the semester Christmas party? These questions may help you identify examples of problems that you have solved. Consider the following: what choices did you make, why did you make them and what was the result?

It's funny. No one ever comes in and asks me whether an RA position should go on their résumé, or whether it is relevant. They assume it is. Christians, on the other hand, come into my office and say, "I led a Bible study, is that relevant?" No. It's not. The company is not hiring Bible study leaders. But they're not hiring Resident Assistants at their company either. You need to talk about transferable skills like *problem-solving*.

"I was a small group leader and we had the difficult task of growing attendance for our weekly meeting. I was able to ask some analytical questions regarding what nights of the week work best for students based on other campus activities. In addition, I identified high traffic areas to advertise our group. Recognizing that retention is as important as recruitment, I made sure that our meetings were fun and welcoming. You could say we wanted more customers, but we also wanted *loyal* customers."

The fact that it was a Bible study needs not be mentioned. It's not irreverent to call it a small group because it was, in fact, small, and a group. You will be working with small groups of people in my company, but you likely won't be leading a Bible study, at least not on the clock.

Of course, you can tailor this to whatever kind of job you are seeking— education, marketing, social work, etc. Just remember these three takeaways:

1. As a person of faith, you rely on analytical skills all of the time to develop a robust and reasonable faith.
2. The skills you use in "ministry" are general skills that are used by everyone. Why would yours be less relevant just because you developed them or used them in a faith-based context?
3. We are just scratching the surface here, but I trust that you can use your problem-solving skills to bring these ideas into your personal context.

# FOR REFLECTION

Since you are a problem solver you will want to let employers know that. The challenge many people have in doing that is that they haven't taken the time to consider examples of how they have solved problems. Take some time right now to look at the list of topics that you created in the introduction and for each one identify problems that you solved. Remember, since you are constantly solving problems you probably don't even think about it. For example, a freshman needs a ride to your Bible study on the other side of campus. You can 1) ask her to walk and be a few minutes late, 2) go pick her up and be late because you are also picking up others, or 3) call a student who you know is near the freshman and ask them to pick her up. Begin to identify and write down examples from your own experiences.

# COMPETENCY
# TWO

## ORAL & WRITTEN COMMUNICATIONS

*"Articulate thoughts and ideas clearly and effectively in written and oral forms to persons inside and outside of the organization. The individual has public speaking skills; is able to express ideas to others; and can write/edit memos, letters, and complex technical reports clearly and effectively."* \*

**THE MAN THREW HIS HANDS** in the air and said, "I literally just need someone who can write a professional email with more than 140 characters without using text talk like *LOL*." This was the response I received after asking an employer what he meant by "needing written communication skills." His was not an uncommon response.

I've already mentioned that analytical skills are fundamental to our faith because we largely draw from a written text for our understanding of who God is. We believe that this is how he has chosen to preserve his words for us today. Written communication is, in fact, revered in the Christian faith. In addition, much of the biblical text that we hold today was originally preserved through memorization and oral communication. Thus, within our faith context, we value those too.

\* naceweb.org/career-readiness/competencies/career-readiness-defined/

As I mentioned previously, I work as a career coach for a state university. Within that context, I regularly have appointments with students who are involved in Christian ministries on campus. Occasionally students will come into my office for me to review their résumés. Along with other activities, they will list, "Mission trip to XYZ." I typically advise them to add some value statements with this.

I'll ask, "What did you do on this trip?"

"Nothing relevant to the job."

"Why is it on here then?"

"Okay, I'll take it off." (Why are we so quick to take it off? It's like we are hoping for someone to think our ministry experiences are worthless.)

"No!" I say, "What did you do on the trip?"

(Keep in mind that not all of these students know that I'm a Christian.)

Sheepishly, "We shared the gospel."

"How did you do that?"

"We walked around and talked to people and asked them about their lives. If they had time, we would sit down and tell them about Jesus. And we would invite them to our events."

"Did anyone ever say they weren't interested?"

With a sense of failure, head slightly down, a mumbled "Yes."

Consider it this way: If you had a spring break opportunity that allowed you to do a day's worth of intense sales training, and then do a week-long intensive that required you to go door to door and sell the product, would you list it on your résumé? If so, why? What skills do you think you would have gained? Let me suggest a few:

1. You probably had to craft a written sales pitch that you memorized and said over and over to real people.
2. You probably learned how to deal with some rejection.
3. You probably developed people skills while talking with strangers.

How is this different from that mission trip? Why is it so easy to bring up sales training in your interview and so hard to bring up missions? In an interview, you are likely not going to tell them everything you know and memorized about the cable provider that you were selling. Right? You are going to talk about the skills that you developed. Couldn't this be true of missions? You just need to take the *Christianese* out of your vocabulary. Not everyone knows what you mean by "the gospel" so how else might you talk about your experience on the trip?

And what about discipleship? Do you ever grab coffee on campus with someone that you mentor in the faith? Or someone that came to your large weekly meeting and then requested more information about your group? These meetings are honing your communication skills in a way that few other student organizations do. Christian ministry is a substantial training ground for the oral communication skills for which employers are looking.

Written communication skills are critical as well. The ministries with which I have been involved have utilized a significant amount of email communication (or Slack, etc.) for planning and announcements. If you are producing this content, be sure to highlight this skill to employers. If you are the one who is easily annoyed by the flood of emails and fail to read them or read them thoroughly, or if you are often jeered for your spelling errors, perhaps you should think of it differently. These are not just inconveniences in your otherwise efficient day (read a hint of sarcasm), rather they are opportunities to develop a highly regarded skill that you will be using in the workplace for the rest of your life.

Recognize also that the letter you wrote to raise funds for your mission trip was a critical example of written communication. So were the update emails that you sent while you were on the trip, and the thank-you letter that you wrote when you returned. Don't hesitate to mention that you raised $2000 for a trip through written communication and then updated your support team throughout the event week. If you can do that for a week-long trip, you can likely use that same skill to make my company more profitable or raise funds for my non-profit agency.

# FOR REFLECTION

1. What are some examples of ways that you have used written and oral communication?

2. Where or under what circumstances did you develop or grow in these skills?

3. Who can you rely on to help you improve your oral and written skills or to edit your work?

4. Remember, your résumé and social media platforms are samples of your written communication skills. Make sure they are free of typos and grammatical errors.

# COMPETENCY
# THREE

## TEAMWORK/ COLLABORATION

*"Build collaborative relationships with colleagues and customers representing diverse cultures, races, ages, genders, religions, lifestyles, and viewpoints. The individual is able to work within a team structure and can negotiate and manage conflict."* \*

**"HAVE YOU EVER BEEN ON** *a team, and someone wasn't pulling their weight?"* This is a popular interview question. Employers call it a *behavioral* interview question. These types of questions require you to tell a story about how you have acted in a particular situation. Employers ask these types of questions because the best predictor of future behavior is past behavior. If you can tell me how you have resolved conflict with your classmates during a group project, then I will have a pretty good idea of how you might relate with the team that I put you on in my company.

I hope that when you read the description of the competency above, you immediately related it to the values within your Christian faith. When my wife and I first became Christians during our college years, certain interrelational values were drilled into us. I suppose because we were in a group of other ambitious young people that were rough around the edg-

\* naceweb.org/career-readiness/competencies/career-readiness-defined/

es, conflict was bound to happen. Our mentors were at the ready to use these conflicts as a training ground.

- "How is it that you see the speck of sawdust in your brother's eye and pay no attention to the plank in your own eye?" (*Matthew 7:3, Luke 6:41*)
- "Do not let the sun go down while you are still angry." (*Ephesians 4:26*)
- If someone sins against *you*, approach *them*. (*Matthew 18:15-20*)
- Turn the other cheek, walk an extra mile, give them your tunic...'er, coat. (*Matthew 5:38-42*)
- Love your neighbor *as* yourself. (*Matthew 22:36-40*)

There are many more, but these just rolled through my head. They are messages of humility, generosity, forgiveness, reconciliation, and restoration. I mean, come on, Jesus is the perfect example of all of this—*the* servant-leader.

But in the NACE definition, there is all that language about diversity. Yep, that sounds like the call of the Christian, doesn't it?

- Love your neighbor as yourself (there it is again)
- To Abraham, God said, "...and through your offspring all nations of the earth will be blessed" (*Genesis 26:4*)
- "Then all nations will be blessed through him, and they will call him blessed." (*Psalm 72:17*)
- There is no distinction between man and woman, Jew and gentile, etc. (*Ephesians 2:11-22; Galatians 3:28-29*)
- When the Church was created at Pentecost, men from many nations were there and said, "Aren't all these who are speaking Galileans? Then how is it that each of us hears them in our native language? ...[W]e hear them declaring the wonders of God in our own tongues!" (*Acts 2:7-11*)
- How about that first really diverse church in Antioch to which Paul was called to teach (*Acts 11:19-26*)?

Themes of loving all people, treating people with dignity, and sharing a common humanity are all woven into the very fabric of the Church. My point is that the principles emphasized under the rubric of Team/Collaboration are ones that, as a Christian, you should already hold to. Healthy conflict resolution? Non-negotiable. Diversity? Absolutely.

Have you ever had to personally work through resolving a conflict with another member of your ministry team? What about those whom you lead? Have you ever helped others through conflict-resolution, maybe members of a small group or roommates? How about a road trip to a service project? You get humans in a car for more than an hour, and someone's going to need forgiveness.

Diversity? It's a value; but do you have examples? Does your ministry host international students for holiday meals? Do you have a conversational English group? Have you traveled anywhere for a cross-cultural trip? (Yes, missions count.)

Of the eight secret ingredients, this one is likely the most obvious as to how it relates to your Christian values. This is good news for you because it is critically important to employers and the world of work.

# FOR REFLECTION

1. Tell about a project on which you collaborated with others.

2. Tell about a time that you worked with a diverse group (for example, different ages, races, ethnicities, disabilities, etc.).

3. Tell about a time that you resolved an interpersonal conflict and how you demonstrated courage and grace in addressing the issue.

# COMPETENCY
# FOUR

## DIGITAL
## TECHNOLOGY

*"Leverage existing digital technologies ethically and efficiently to solve problems, complete tasks, and accomplish goals. The individual demonstrates effective adaptability to new and emerging technologies."* *

**AS YOU KNOW, DIGITAL TECHNOLOGY** has been important since the beginning of time. Exhibit A: Eve had an Apple. Ok, please don't stop reading! That was a terrible joke and completely biblically inaccurate. Eve ate an unspecified "fruit." Which just goes to show you that there will always be some critics hate'n on Apple. (Ok, now I will stop.)

Seriously though, you may be asking, "What does digital technology have to do with my faith?" Well, let's start simply with the technology part. Technology is a product of people who were created to create. How long do you think it took for Adam, in caring for the garden, before he thought, "You know Eve, this would be easier if we had some tools."? We were designed as co-creators. God placed us in the garden and told us to make stuff with what he had already made (*Genesis 1:28*). Perhaps one of the most prominent examples of this is when God provided the gifts for the makers of the temple (*Exodus 31:1-11*). Christians have valued using re-

* naceweb.org/career-readiness/competencies/career-readiness-defined/

sources to serve the world throughout history. Think of the hospitals built in order to use medical technology to care for the sick. Or the schools that have been built to use resources to educate children. Just this past year I was in a conversation with a friend who serves on the board of a non-profit that aims to alleviate homelessness in a major city. They have created a system that can get a homeless person from anywhere in the city to available food and shelter within minutes. They have accomplished this by using existing Google products that we all use every day to map the resources and hours of operation of the many organizations within the city and bring a collective order to a web of disconnected services. Technology can be a force for good.

In the NACE definition of this competency, there are a few critical components that are worth mentioning.

**First, problem solving.** We already talked about this, so I won't add much here other than to say as Christians we value problem solving.

**Second, the word "ethically."** Perhaps this should be more obvious than it is, but Christians of all people should hold ethical work in high regard. After all, we are not looking out for just ourselves but also for the good of others (*Philippians 2:4*), we are not working only for personal gain (*1 Thessalonians 2:4*) and we are serving God not man (*Ephesians 6:6-8*). We should be the annoyingly consistent example of ethical behavior.

**Third, "effective adaptability."** The challenge that many people have with technology is that by the time they master something, they are already behind the times on new technologies. Adaptability can be frustrating, perhaps especially for "old" people like me. I think this is because the learning of technology is often seen as an unnecessary obstacle in the way of actually getting their work done. However, if the employer is saying, "Hey, I want you to know and understand how to use this new technology" then that is the work (or part of it). This is an area where some of us need to give ourselves permission to be curious. Learning agility is valued in every field.

After all, the biblical worldview is one that sees the richness of creation as a beautiful invitation to explore every square inch, yet never in all of our searching get bored by exhausting our possibilities.

Are you using technology to manage programs in your student ministry? Perhaps Google products such as Drive for collaborating on content, Sheets for working collectively on budgets or schedules, Slides for preparing a missions presentation, Meet for connecting with a team or Maps for charting your trip? As it turns out, you probably are already enjoying the efficiencies of certain tools. And, as it turns out, employers want that.

# FOR REFLECTION

It's important to remember here to not step into the "I'm not techy" trap. Generally speaking, employers do not need you to be a software developer. They simply need people who can get comfortable using everyday technology and learn new ones when necessary.

1. What software do you use? Why? How? (for example, Zoom for video conferencing, Word for writing papers, Google Sheets for planning trips,etc.)

2. What apps do you use? Why? How?

3. What non-software technology do you use? Why? How? (for example, sound boards, video equipment, etc.)

4. What social media do you use? Do you use different platforms for different purposes? (for example, SnapChat v. LinkedIn) Remember, employers look at your media too. Be mindful of what you post regardless of the platform.

# COMPETENCY
# FIVE

## LEADERSHIP

*"Leverage the strengths of others to achieve common goals, and use interpersonal skills to coach and develop others. The individual is able to assess and manage his/her emotions and those of others; use empathetic skills to guide and motivate; and organize, prioritize, and delegate work."* \*

**LEADERSHIP IS OFTEN MISUNDERSTOOD.** We tend to hold up some caricature of a leader and then decide if we want to be that. More times than not, the answer is no. If you are reading about personality types, there seems to be one type that is more of that dominant, up-front kind of person. The image for that person seems to always be in a power suit and tie, standing behind a podium. The caricatures of the other personalities are more interesting to the majority of people (because only a fraction of the population likes standing behind a podium). The artist with her paint brush, the adventurer with his hiking boots and backpack, the investigator with her spy kit. Name the personality test, and there are similar images.

The tragic downside to this is that it implies that artists, adventures, investigators, etc. aren't or can't be leaders. This is absolutely not true. I like NACE's description above because it debunks some of that nonsense. It

\* naceweb.org/career-readiness/competencies/career-readiness-defined/

describes leadership as being able to foster the strengths in others and organize in such a way that others thrive in their strengths—all of this being done with empathy and emotional intelligence.

Not surprisingly, the results of the research that NACE has done line up with the worldview that the scripture teaches. The scriptural examples of leadership include the understanding that everyone has been given gifts *(1 Corinthians 12:7)*, that leadership is not about stature *(1 Samuel 16)*, that we are to have lives that build into others *(2 Timothy 2:2 )*, that we are to be people of humility putting others first *(Philippians 2:3-4)*, and that we are to do so with emotional intelligence *(Numbers 20)*. There are loads of leadership lessons throughout scripture; rich passages like the fruit of the spirit in Galatians 5. Simply looking at the life of the one we call our leader, King Jesus. Humility. Integrity. Investing in others through relationship. Empathy. Delegation (he gave the ultimate example of turning his organization over to those he raised up). I could go on and on.

When students come into my office, and they have a student organization listed on their résumé, I always ask what their role was in the organization. I often get the answer, "I am *just* a member." We could spend a long time unpacking this answer. But let me make just a couple of observations.

There is a difference between *positions* and *roles*. Positions in organizations come with titles. These positions are limited, not everyone gets one, they are often taken by upperclassmen, and they are usually by a vote which is out of your control. *Roles,* on the other hand, are almost entirely in your hands. For instance, when I ask students, "What do you mean you are a 'member' of the XYZ Club?" They will often say something like, "I just attend some meetings to listen to speakers. I joined because I knew it would look good on my résumé." What an employer hears in this is, "I am a spectator." But they are not looking for spectators. Having XYZ Club on your résumé is only helpful if you have gained something or contributed something, and this doesn't mean you need a title. The answer could have just as easily been, *"As a member, I show up early to help the officers set up the room, which also gives me the opportunity to greet guests as they arrive. I specifically like to focus on first-time attendees to help them feel welcome. In addition, I invite others from my residence hall and classes, so that they can also benefit from our programs. In the future, I would like to have an official position in the club, but right now I am establishing myself as a leader by serving those around me."* In that answer I hear emotional intelligence, motivation, interpersonal skills, common goals, servanthood, prioritization, time management, and organization. I hear *leadership*. If your club happens to be a student ministry, this all still applies.

In addition to the "club" aspect, student ministries also often have summer leadership training programs, leadership retreats, conferences, and spring break experiences. These are all great places to develop as a leader. They are not categorically different from other clubs on campus in terms of developing the kinds of leaders that employers need. In fact, most campus ministries are more robust because their advisors and mentors are seasoned leaders and are far more engaged with the group.

You need to learn how to talk about your leadership experiences in ways that relate to the jobs you are seeking. By this, I mean tone down the insider language and talk about the transferable aspects of what you have done. Continue to work through the reflection questions in each section. By putting in the intentional work now, you will develop the ability to talk readily about your story in ways that resonate with employers.

The world needs more leaders that display the servant-leadership qualities of Jesus. Who better to offer this than those who hold to his teachings?

# FOR REFLECTION

1. What leadership titles have you had, if any? What were your assigned duties? Is there an example of when you went above and beyond what was being asked of you?

2. When have you led without a title? Describe what you did?

3. Have you ever been a part of a leadership training experience? What was that like? (This could be a few hours or a whole summer.)

# COMPETENCY
# SIX

## PROFESSIONALISM/
## WORK ETHIC

*"Demonstrate personal accountability and effective work habits, e.g., punctuality, working productively with others, and time workload management, and understand the impact of non-verbal communication on professional work image. The individual demonstrates integrity and ethical behavior, acts responsibly with the interests of the larger community in mind, and is able to learn from his/her mistakes." \**

**WHEN I WAS IN COLLEGE,** I spent a summer with a campus ministry in Myrtle Beach for a leadership training program. The program had a partnership with a grocery store chain that allowed us to supply their seasonal staffing needs.

On the first day of the program, the campus ministry staff met with the several hundred students attending the program and laid out some guidelines regarding our work expectations and then collected our applications for employment. The talk, in part, went something like this: "This grocery franchise partners with us because we provide them with quality employees. This is because as Christians we believe that we should be the best employees that they hire. This is because we work for an audience of one,

* naceweb.org/career-readiness/competencies/career-readiness-defined/

God (*Colossians 3:17*). This means we don't steal a single paper clip, or pen, and we don't steal time. If our shift ends at 5 p.m., we do not leave the floor until 5 p.m. We do not line up at the time clock 15 minutes before 5 p.m. waiting to clock out. That's their time. They are paying us to work."

There was more to it, but this is the part that I remember. I had just started following Jesus, and it was a foundational message to me. "Your beliefs should impact your work." We learned a lot of lessons that summer through weekly meetings and beach outreaches, but over 20 years later, this is the lesson that I remember.

As a result of that basic introduction to a Christian perspective of work, I have always been perplexed when others don't see it that way. I am most discouraged when people use the idea of Christian liberty as a license to do whatever they want or to treat people however they want. Or when Christian students say things like, "Well, that business was all about money. Clearly, I didn't want to work at a place like that, so I walked out."

I believe this is a misuse of Christian liberty. Sure, it is for freedom that Christ set us free *(Galatians 5:1)*, but not in order for us to do whatever we want *(Romans 6:1)*. Jesus was the most differentiated person that ever walked the earth. He was freed by the absolute understanding of his own identity as a child of God and his purpose on this earth, but he did not hold that over anyone's head. He showed unprecedented humility and served others *(Philippians 2:1–11)*.

Look again at the description above that NACE provides for Professionalism/Work Ethic. Is there anyone on the planet that this should resonate with more than people who follow the teachings of Jesus?

Christians should not be in the game of separating "spiritual" work and "secular" work and then making judgments on how they should approach it. *All* work is sacred. God provided mankind with the joy of work from *before* the fall. Work, therefore, is not a result of sin; it is not due to the curse. And as we read Jeremiah's exhortation to exiled Israel in *Jeremiah 29:4–7*, we find that there is no deviation from the cultural mandate of *Genesis 1:28*. We have excellent examples, like those of Joseph and Daniel, of working unto God in "secular" organizations.

As someone who has worked with many college students, I believe this same professionalism should be applied to school. It is the ideal practice field for developing a good work ethic. Unfortunately, the predominant attitude among many college students is, "this is *just* college." As if college is some middle world between being a kid and being an adult.

Perhaps we forget that the Josephs and Daniels of scripture were likely college-age. I suppose the difference is that you are paying for college rather than being paid. However, as consumers, we are typically pretty adamant about getting what we pay for. If you order an 8-piece nugget and receive only 7, someone needs to make it right. College is expensive. Why do we treat it differently? *(Full disclosure: when I was in college I treated it differently too.)*

If you want to get the most bang for your buck and *really* prepare yourself for the world of work, treat school like it's something to which you are called rather than a detour on the road *to* your calling. Your education is sacred work too, done for an audience of one.

# FOR REFLECTION

1. Do you see your role as a student as a calling? Take time to reflect on why or why not?

2. What changes would you make if you believed that school was your calling from God and you were to do all things unto him? (Maybe you already do.)

3. Do you see your current job as a calling? Would you change anything if you did?

# COMPETENCY
# SEVEN

## CAREER MANAGEMENT

*"Identify and articulate one's skills, strengths, knowledge, and experiences relevant to the position desired and career goals, and identify areas necessary for professional growth. The individual is able to navigate and explore job options, understands and can take the steps necessary to pursue opportunities, and understands how to self-advocate for opportunities in the workplace."* \*

**UNDERSTANDING ONE'S STRENGTHS AND SKILLS** is something that many churches regularly promote. Perhaps your church provides "spiritual gift assessments" as part of their membership class or leadership development. Or maybe your small group or leadership team has taken a personality assessment like MBTI or the Enneagram. Christians tend to understand that the Bible teaches that individuals are given gifts *(1 Corinthians 12)* and that God created us uniquely to do good works which God prepared for us *(Psalm 139:13-18, Ephesians 2:10)*. These assessments are helpful to give us perspective on the types of tasks in which *we* should be investing and the kind of tasks that are probably better yielded to others.

\* naceweb.org/career-readiness/competencies/career-readiness-defined/

In addition, the Church has a strong emphasis on personal growth. My guess is that every week someone in your church or student ministry provides a message that concludes with specific applications aimed at helping you to grow personally and spiritually. The Christian life is not one of complacency but one of continual development.

This same understanding should be applied to our professional careers. Our jobs are one of the primary places that we get to live out our gifts. Employers, like ministries, want to place people to serve in functional areas in which they can do their best work and consequently enjoy the process of growing, improving, and applying their skills to new opportunities. The NACE definition speaks of "self-advocacy." This is to say that we don't sit on our hands and hope something comes our way. Instead, we look at potential future opportunities, discover how to develop the necessary skills to do a good job, and then ask for the responsibility.

It is unlikely that you think of your Christian life in terms of career management. However, this competency aligns with what most Christians are learning in the church: grow, learn, develop, and look for a place to serve rather than to be served.

As a career coach, I see two interview questions trip up people in ways that directly relate to this competency:

1.  What are three of your weaknesses (and strengths)?
2.  What are your future goals/where do you see yourself in five years?

Most students for whom I provide practice interviews answer these questions from a defensive position, i.e., they don't want to mess up. The significance of the career management competency, however, should challenge candidates to come at these questions from a place of strength and confidence.

Employers know that you have weaknesses. Don't try to hide them. Think of the weakness question (and all questions) in relation to the job description and let them know what skill areas you need to grow in. Then trust that they will respect your self-awareness and train you where needed. This is to your advantage as well. You don't want to get hired after not being honest, only to discover that the company isn't equipped to develop you and find yourself doomed to work in a position for which you are not skilled.

Employers also want to know that you understand various paths forward in your career. When they ask about your five-year plan, they don't expect you to know the future. However, you can demonstrate to them that you have done some reflecting, and that you know some options exist within their company. Students often do harm to their efforts when answering this question while interviewing for internships. They'll say, "I would like to have this internship because it will look good on my résumé when I apply for a full-time position at another company." If that company hires for their full-time positions out of their intern pool (as many do), then they are likely to be looking for interns who want to work for them long term. So, tell them the kind of career path that you are looking for and ask them if they can provide that opportunity. They will appreciate your "self-advocacy" per the definition above.

The bottom line is that, as Christians, we are to live intentional lives. Lives of purpose. Career Management is part of this. Your career is your responsibility. Think about who you are, what you have to offer, and create a flexible plan of potential paths forward.

# FOR REFLECTION

1. Have you ever considered what career paths exist in your field? Take time now to write down a few possible paths. If you do not know any it would be a good idea to talk with someone in the field to gain understanding of this.

2. Good news! You don't have to have it all figured out! None of us know what we want the next five years to look like exactly. Think of it this way: what paths are you curious about exploring in the next few years? Take a moment now to write down some ideas.

3. Do you know your strengths and weaknesses? What are some things you like doing?

4. How have you grown in specific areas? Where would you like to see more growth?

5. Remember, it is important to research a company before an interview. This will allow you to learn about what growth opportunities exist within their organization. Use this information to ask informed questions about potential career paths.

# COMPETENCY
# EIGHT

## GLOBAL/INTERCULTURAL
## FLUENCY

*"Value, respect, and learn from diverse cultures, races, ages, genders, sexual orientations, and religions. The individual demonstrates openness, inclusiveness, sensitivity, and the ability to interact respectfully with all people and understand individuals' differences." ***

**THIS IS THE FINAL COMPETENCY** that NACE lists in their report. It is the last but certainly not least. As I began writing this chapter, I had to pause. Global and Intercultural Fluency is at the very core of a biblical worldview. Because of that, this chapter should be easy to write. There are plenty of examples that are easy to apply here. In many ministries, however, a lot of intercultural work has been done with good intentions and yet with damaging results. The key to walking through this is to start where NACE's definition starts: "value, respect, and learn from diverse cultures." Too often missions, whether local or abroad, have been done with little intention of learning from other cultures and the root of this is unfortunately a lack of respect and value for others.

* naceweb.org/career-readiness/competencies/career-readiness-defined/

You may think it seems contradictory to think that you can do missions without valuing or respecting others. After all, missions take a great deal of sacrifice and intentionality so we might conclude that this comes from a place of value and respect for others. Historically, this has not always been the case. A great deal of missions has been done from a desire to "fix" or "rescue" others without actually giving time to understanding them. I do not have time to dive into the deep end on this topic. If you would like more, I suggest that you pick up a copy of *When Helping Hurts* by Brian Fikkert and Steve Corbett.

I am assuming here that the motives of missions come from a place of valuing, respecting, and seeking to understand others. I believe this is supported by the biblical text and is perhaps seen most evident in Paul's approaches to missions in each of his sermons in Acts. Paul takes the time to understand his audience and what they value,—this is evidenced in the way he tailors his messages—but the ultimate picture of this is, of course, Jesus himself who "did not consider equality with God something to be used to his own advantage...taking on the very nature of a servant, being made in human likeness" *(Philippians 2:6-7)*. These are not simply ministry strategies, they are genuine desires to understand others.

Assuming these are the underpinning motives, there are lots of examples of global and intercultural activities within student ministries and churches that have likely prepared you well for the workplace. Here are just a few that come to mind:

- Short-term international mission trip
- Short-term domestic mission trip for a service project
- Conversational English class with international students
- International student meals
- Trips to nursing homes
- Serving as a mentor to another student from a different background

These activities typically come with some training regarding how to love someone who is different than ourselves.

In my work as a career coach, I have found that students, more times than not, do not take the time to consider how to translate their missions activities in a way that makes sense in the general employment world. For instance, when communicating about a mission trip to Africa over spring break, students will list evangelism and Vacation Bible School (VBS) on their résumés. When I ask more specific questions about these activities I learn that "evangelism" involved the student meeting strangers for coffee and talking about their culture and their worldview. "VBS" meant that they organized a soccer camp for children ages 8-15 and followed the practices with a prepared values-based curriculum where they discussed things like honesty, integrity, empathy, and courage.

The students that I work with have grown as individuals after having seen and talked to people that do not have the economic opportunities that an average American does. They are humbled by another culture's extreme hospitality and value of family. They are struck by the joy of the children and their eagerness to learn, and they are saddened that the children do not have what we may consider basic resources for learning.

All of these outcomes display a rich intercultural fluency that an employer wants in an employee. Therefore, a résumé needs to touch on the transferable skills and provoke questions that will allow the applicant to talk more about the value of his or her cultural experience in an interview. "Evangelism" and "Vacation Bible School" will likely not provoke this dialogue and could potentially stir a negative response.

As I mentioned earlier, the job search process, which includes cover letters, résumés, interviews, networking and thank-you cards, is really about the art of storytelling. When you consider your global or intercultural experiences, keep asking yourself questions like, *What did I learn from this? How did I grow? Why was this meaningful?* or *How am I different as a result?* These are the stories that you need to tell.

Understand the context in which you are telling these stories. The employer wants to know "If I put you on a team of people who aren't like you, how will you respond?" Or, "If you have to interact with clients who are different from you (which you will), how will you treat them?" You are not telling stories about how you are the hero that came in and saved the day by building a house or giving away shoes. You are telling stories about how, having had the experience that you did, you are now more equipped with empathy, patience, humility, and listening skills than you were before.

Here's an example to consider. Let's say you are on an international mission trip and you are the designated photographer. When you return you have some pictures of your team but you also have lots of pictures of the locals that you served. Think through the photos of children and their parents. What is that child's story? Is there anything that saddens you? Is there anything that encourages you? What will you be praying for them in the years to come? In what way would you like to be more like them? In what way are you more fortunate than them? What are they thankful for? What are you thankful for? Working through exercises like this with your own global and intercultural experiences will help you get away from the "what did I do" question and move towards the "how did it change me for the better" question.

We live in a global society and it is critical that employees are able to function well within it.

This is not just an employment value. It is a biblical one.

# FOR REFLECTION

1. Identify three to five examples of when you have worked with diverse populations. What did you learn during those opportunities?

2. Reflect on your perspective before and after these experiences. Did your perspective change as a result of these opportunities? In what way?

# CONCLUSION

## WHERE TO FROM HERE?

*"The Great King has summoned each of us into his throne room. 'Take this portion of my kingdom', he says, 'I am making you my steward over your office, your workbench, your kitchen stove. Put your heart into mastering this part of my world. Get it in order, unearth its treasures; do all you can with it. Then everyone will see what a glorious King I am.' That's why we get up every morning and go to work. We don't labor simply to survive, insects do that. Our work is an honor, a privileged commission from our great King. God has given each of us a portion of his kingdom to explore and to develop to its fullness."* —**Richard Pratt, *Designed for Dignity***

**HOPEFULLY, THIS REFLECTION GUIDE HAS** been a helpful resource for you as you consider the value of your experiences and their application to your future aspirations. As you go forward from here, I encourage you to consider the quote above and think about the current spaces in which you find yourself—classrooms, research labs, residence halls, study lounges, on-campus jobs, etc. What would it look like to put your heart into mastering the areas over which you have been made a steward? As a student, it can be tempting to put this off until you are "in the real world." But you *are* in the real world. There is no better place to form meaningful disciplines than where we find ourselves in the present. And, each day you and I can wake up and embrace the privileged commission that we have been given and live our lives joyfully unto the glorious King.

If you would like to spend some intentional time with others considering life and vocation check out **Muncie Fellows** (MuncieFellows.com), a nine-month leadership program that equips college graduates to live out their faith in every area of life, or consider one of the many other Fellows programs throughout the country through **The Fellows Initiative** network (TheFellowsInitiative.org).

**For a deeper dive into the subject of vocation, here are a few book recommendations:**

- *Every Good Endeavor: Connecting Your Work to God's Work* by Timothy Keller with Katherine Leary Alsdorf

- *How Then Should We Work?: Rediscovering the Biblical Doctrine of Work* by Hugh Whelchel

- *Ready or Not: Leaning into Life in Our Twenties* by Drew Moser and Jess Fankhauser

*Steady on,*
*Jeff Eads*

# ABOUT THE AUTHOR

 Jeff Eads has the unique perspective of having spent decades working with college students and young professionals. He has held positions at both a state university and a small Christian university and he has held full-time positions in both support-based college ministry and in a traditional church.

Jeff currently serves as a career coach and the Associate Director of Employer Relations and Recruitment Programs at Ball State University. He also serves as co-Executive Director for the Muncie Fellows, a nine-month leadership program that equips college graduates to live out their faith in every area of life.

Jeff has spoken throughout the country at professional conferences, college retreats, and in the classroom on topics ranging from professional development to living missionally.

# ENDORSEMENTS

Christian college students who are not looking to work in official ministry jobs often wrestle with how their faith informs what they are pursuing in their professional life. They may know theoretically that all work matters to the Lord but it is often hard to tangibly picture what that looks like in their specific context. In *Qualified*, Jeff Eads brilliantly gives practical examples of how ministry experience prepares Christians for work in any industry. His words will encourage and empower Christian students to confidently pursue careers in all professional spheres and also be about kingdom renewal in the workplace.

**Jonathan Ingraham**
Executive Director, Chattanooga Faith + Work + Culture

As someone who has experience working in both the corporate world and the ministry world, I can attest to Jeff Eads's argument that the skill sets developed in ministry can absolutely translate into the business world. Jeff does an outstanding job of layering the NACE requirements with the various Christian experiences of college students. It is my hope and prayer that this book will be the catalyst for students to shine the Light of Jesus into the corporate world.

**Tim Beatty**
President of Bullen Ultrasonics, Inc.

Jeff Eads has written a must-read primer for anyone wanting to demonstrate that their ministry experience has produced invaluable life skills.

**Alexander Lowry**
Professor of Finance, Executive Director of Career &
Connection Institute, Gordon College

Made in the USA
Columbia, SC
28 January 2021